A COLLECTION

OF

Proverbs and Popular Sayings

RELATING TO

THE SEASONS, THE WEATHER, AND AGRICULTURAL PURSUITS;

GATHERED CHIEFLY FROM ORAL TRADITION.

BY

M. A. DENHAM.

MDCCCXLVI.

COUNCIL

OF

The Percy Society.

————

PREFACE.

To those who are aware of the time and trouble
required for the accumulation of any extensive
series of traditional sayings, it will cause no sur-
prise to be informed, that the present Collection
was commenced as far back as the year 1825. In
the following year, I sent half-a-dozen (probably
all that I had then collected) to Mr. William Hone,
for insertion in the *Every-Day Book*, then in course
of publication. In that work they did not appear;
but were printed in vol. ii. col. 505, of his succeeding periodical (*The Table-Book*), along with
other matter, subscribed with the initials of my
name reversed. From this period, the collection
went on gradually increasing till the year 1843;
when having collected, chiefly orally, upwards of
four hundred, I made a selection therefrom, which

I arranged for insertion in the *Local Historian's
Table-Book*, a work of no common merit, edited
by Mr. M. A. Richardson, of Newcastle-on-Tyne.
These, with few or no foot-notes, appeared in
vol. ii. pp. 211 and 254, in the *Traditional* portion
of the above publication. "As a token of friend-
ship," Mr. M. A. R. struck off twenty-five copies
in a distinct form, which, with the exception of
two or three copies which I still retain, have been
distributed among my own especial friends, and
three or four of the members of the Percy Society;
one of whom was so kind (I being a total stranger
to him) as to offer his services, not only to submit
the same to the consideration of the Council of
the Society, but, likewise, to honour me with his
valuable services in adding thereto from foreign,
and more ancient English manuscript and printed
collections. I have acted upon his suggestion;
and with his able assistance I can have nothing
to fear.

Although the Collector has never seen a single
copy either of Howell's, Ray's, Kelly's, Fuller's, or
Henderson's Proverbs, he has slight hesitation in
asserting that, after the most careful collation,
many—very many—will be found in this collection
which are not to be found in any other, either
printed, or in manuscript. To him it has been a
treasure constantly accumulating: few weeks pass-

ing over but one or more have been added to the
mass of provincial literature. Like the Lambton
worm, of northern celebrity,—

> " It grew, it grew, and still it grew;"

or the *Pilgrim's Progress* of poor old John
Bunyan,—

> " ———— Until, at last, it came to be,
> For length and breadth, the bigness which you see."

The remarks of Mr. Brand, when noticing
"*vulgar* RITES and *popular opinions*," are equally
applicable to PROVERBS, viz.: "They have indeed
travelled down to us through a long succession of
years, and the greater part of them, it is not im-
probable, will be of perpetual observation: for the
generality of men look back with superstitious
veneration on the ages of their forefathers; and
matters that are grey with time, seldom fail of
commanding those filial honours claimed even by
the appearance of hoary age."

" If before ye knew only these things, be not
disgusted because I have inserted them; if ye
shall know more, be not angry that I have not
spoken of them, but rather let him communicate
his knowledge to me, while I yet live, that, at
least, those things may appear in the margin of
my book, which do not occur in the text."—
Guliel. de Malms.

Finally : having made use of my best endeavours to make this an offering worthy of the acceptance of the members of the Percy Society, I may, perhaps, be permitted to conclude in the words of another and more ancient writer: "And if I have *done well*, and as is fitting the story, *it is that which I desired*; but if SLENDERLY and MEANLY, it is that which I could attain unto."

M. AISLABIE DENHAM.

Pierse Bridge, near Darlington,
24th August, 1846.

GENERAL ADAGES, PROVERBS,

ETC.

A FOG cannot be dispelled with a fan.
Plough or plough not, you must pay your rent.*
Many drops make a shower.
Ill weeds grow apace.
Tomorrow is untouched.
Further East, the shorter West.
Say no ill of the year till it be past.
Praise a fair day at night.†
Ill weather is seen soon enough when it comes.
A Scotch mist will wet an Englishman to the skin.
Go to bed with the lamb, and rise with the lark.
Blow the wind never so fast, it will lower at last.
It's an ill wind that blows nobody good !‡
Though the sun shines, leave not your coat at home.
If the morning is fine, take your great coat with you;
      if rainy, make your own choice.

---

* A useful hint for the sluggard.
† The Scotch say:—"Roose the fair day at e'en."
‡ See a two-fold illustration of this proverb in Rowland's
Four Knaves, p. 104, under the head of "Harm watch, harm
catch."

Chuse a wife on a Saturday rather than a Sunday.

A new moon soon seen is long thought of.

After a storm comes a calm.

It does not rain but it pours down.

Drought never bred dearth in England.

No weather is ill, if the wind be still.

A green winter makes a fat church-yard.*

Hail brings frost in the tail.

A snow-year—a rich year.†

Winter's thunder is summer's wonder.‡

Frost and fraud both end in foul.

A West wind and an honest man go to bed together.

Good husbandry is good divinity.

Corn and horn go together.§

---

* A mild and open winter is always considered as unhealthy.

† Identical with the German proverb,—*Schnee Jahr, reich Jahr.*

‡ " Thunder and lightning, in winter, in hot countryes, is usual, and hath ye same effects ; but in these northern climates it is held ominous, portending factions, tumults, and bloody wars, and a thing seldome seen, according to the old adigy, 'Winter's thunder is ye sommer's wonder.' "—*Willford's Nature's Secrets,* p. 113.

"Thunders in yᵉ morning signifie wynde; abᵗ noone rayne; in yᵉ evening, great tempest. Somme wryte (yʳ ground I see not) yᵗ Sondaye's thundre should brynge yᵉ death of learned men, judges, and others ; Mondaye's thundre, yᵉ death of women ; Tuesday's thundre, plentie of graine ; Wednesdaye's thundre, yᵉ death of harlotts ; Thursday's thundre, plentie of sheepe and corne ; Fridaie's thundre, yᵉ slaughter of a greate man, and other horrible murders ; Saturdaye's thundre, a generall plague, and grate deathe."—*Leonard Digges' " A Prognostication everlasting of ryght good Effecte,"* &c. 4to. Lond. 1556. Fol. 6. b.

§ *i. e.* when bread is cheap, beef is the same.

Dearth always begins in the horse-manger.

If frogs make a noise in the time of cold rain, warm dry weather will follow.

There is good land where there is a foul way.

After rain, comes fair weather.

An hour in the morning before breakfast, is worth two all the rest of the day.

Never put off till tomorrow, what you can do to-day.

Many a good cow has a bad calf.

An hour's cold will suck out seven years' heat.

Evening oats are good morning fodder.

Flitting of farms makes mailings dear.

Never offer your hen for sale on a rainy day.

Don't let the plough stand to kill a mouse.

Ill weather and sorrow come unsent for.

As the wind blows you must set your sail.

Change of weather is the discourse of fools.

A field requires three things; fair weather, sound seed, and a good husbandman.

Set trees poor, and they will grow rich; set them rich, and they will grow poor.

One hour's sleep before midnight, is worth two after.

In rain and sunshine, cuckolds go to heaven.

Winter thunder, bodes summer hunger.*

As seasonable as snow in summer.

Work to-day, for you know not how much you may be hindered to-morrow.

---

* The Germans have the same proverb,—*Früher donner spater hunger.*

Don't have thy cloak to make when it begins to rain.

Few days pass without some clouds.

They are well off that hav'nt a house to go to.*

The darkest hour is nearest the dawn.

You're saying the ape's pater-noster.†

It is a fine moon, God bless her.‡

When the moon's in the full, then wit's in the wane.

A new moon with sharp horns, threatens windy weather.§

He who carrieth a bay-leaf shall never take harm from thunder.‖

One day is better than sometime a whole year.¶

To dream of little rain and drops of water is good for husbandmen.

The presence of the master is the profit of the field.**

---

* An apposite remark, often quoted by those who sitting comfortably by their "ain ingle side," hear the pelting of the pitiless storm without.

† A kind of proverbial taunt to one whose teeth are chattering with cold.

‡ Brand, on the authority of Bailey, says, "That the common people, in some counties in England, are accustomed to repeat this at the prime of the moon;" and supposes it to proceed from a touch of gentilism, derived from our pagan forefathers.

§ See Brand's *Pop. Antiq.*, ed. Sir Hen. Ellis, vol. iii., p. 74.

‖ See Brand, ib., vol. iii., p. 166.

¶ *Renard the Foxe*, p. 89. *i. e.* "No time—like present time."

** "*Præsentia domini provectus est agri.*"—*Pallad.* lib. i., tit. 6. The eye of the master maketh the ox fat. The eye of the master does more work than his hand. See Herrick's *Hesperides*, ed. by H. G. Clarke. Lond.: 1844. Vol. 2, No. 455, p. 203.

We never know the worth of water till the well is dry.

You gazed at the moon and fell in the gutter.

Small rain will lay a great dust.*

Seven hours' sleep will make the husbandman forget his design.

Stars are not seen by sunshine.

Take time while time is, for time will away.

When the barn is full you may thresh before the door.

When the sun shines nobody minds him; but when he is eclipsed all consider him.

Alike every day, makes a clout on Sunday.

He who does not rise early, never does a good day's work.

The sun is none the worse for shining on a dunghill.

Frost and falsehood have both a dirty gangway.

As the wind blows you must set your sail.

Better have one plough going than two cradles.

Rise early and you will see; wake and you will get wealth.

It is hard to wive and thrive both in one year.

Day and night, sun and moon, air and light, every one must have, but none can buy!

Use not to-day what to-morrow may want.

Wheat will not have two praises.

It rains by planets.

Butter's once a year in the cow's horn.†

---

* A kind answer turneth away wrath.—*Sol.*

† When the cow is *dried* for calving it is usual to say, "All the butter is gone into the cow's horn." Likewise when it is so dear that the poorer classes are unable to purchase it, the same old *dick* is again applicable.

Oysters are never good but in a month that has an R
    in its name.*

Has a Friday look (sulky, downcast).

Bad wintering will tame both man and beast.

Now's now, but Yule's in winter.

Lime makes a rich father and a poor son.†

Neither heat nor cold abides always in the sky.

It's a pity fair weather should ever do harm.

The poor man's labour is the rich man's wealth.

We can say nothing of the day 'till the sun is set.

He never lies but when the hollin's green (holly).

Frost and falsehood never leave a fair hinder end.

After black clouds clear weather.

Change of pasture makes fat calves.

Cloudy mornings turn to clear evenings

Spends Michaelmas rent in Midsummer's moon.‡

He that is mann'd with boys, and hors'd with colts,

Shall have his meat eaten, and his work undone.

It chanceth in an hour that happeneth not in seven
    years.

Make not a balk of good ground.

---

* This proverb accords with the observation made by Butler
in his *Dyet's Dry Dinner*, 1599, viz.: "It is unseasonable and un-
wholesome in all months that have not an R in their name, to eat
an oyster."

† There is no question but that the continual use of lime as
a manure, materially impoverishes any description of soil.

‡ Said of the spendthrift who, fishing before the net, eats the
calf in the cow's belly.

One may see daylight through a small hole.
Of a ragged colt cometh many a good horse.
One scabbed sheep will mar the whole flock.
Puff not against the wind.
God tempers the storm to the shorn lamb.
Grass never grows when the wind blows.
Lose not a hog for a halfpennyworth of tar.

GENERAL PROVERBS IN RHYME.

A SOUTHERLY wind and a cloudy sky,
Proclaim a hunting morning.

A sun-shiny shower,
Won't last half-an-hour.*

In the decay of the moon,
A cloudy morning bodes a fair afternoon.

An evening red and morning grey,
Will set the traveller on his way;†

---

* There are three infantile rhymes used as charms for or against rain, viz.:—

> Rain, rain, go away,
> Come again another day.
> Rain, rain, gang to Spain,
> And never come here again.
> Rain on the green grass, and rain on the tree,
> And rain on the house-top, but not upon me.

It is a highly popular remark in the north, that if as much blue sky is to be seen during rain as will make a pair of *breeches*, the day will "*scarve out;*" *i. e.* it will shortly become fair again.

† The first part of this occurs in German, almost in the same words:—

> "Roth' abend und weisse morgenröth,
> Macht dass der wand'rer freudig geht."

There is a similar proverb in French.

But if the evening's grey, and the morning red,
Put on your hat or you'll wet your head.

A Saturday's moon,
Come when it will it comes too soon.

A rainbow in the morning
Is the shepherd's warning.
A rainbow at night
Is the shepherd's delight.*

Whoso hath but a mouth,
Shall never in England suffer drought.

When the wind doth feed the clay,
England woe and well-a-day;†
But when the clay doth feed the sand,
Then it is well for Angle-land.‡

After a famine in the stall,
Comes a famine in the hall.

---

* It occurs in German with almost the same rhymes:—

> "Regenborgen am morgen
> Macht dem Schäfer sorgen;
> Regenborgen am abend
> Ist dem Schäfer labend."

The French say,

> "L'arc-en-ciel du soir
> Fait beau temps paroir."

† Which is the case in a *wet* summer.
‡ Which is the case in a *dry* summer.

If the cock moult before the hen,
We shall have weather thick and thin;
But if the hen moult before the cock,
We shall have weather hard as a rock.

When the wind is South,
It blows the bait to the fish's mouth.

If there be a rainbow in the eve, it will rain and
    leave;
But if there be a rainbow in the morrow, it
    will neither lend nor borrow.

When the wind's in the East,
It's neither good for man nor beast;
When the wind's in the South,
It's in the rain's mouth.

If the sun in red should set,
The next day surely will be wet;
If the sun should set in grey,
The next will be a rainy day.

The South wind brings wet weather,
The North wind wet and cold together;*
The West wind always brings us rain,
The East wind blows it back again.

---

* A clergyman, in Berkshire, having asked one of his tenants
last week (May 1844), whether he had not better pray for rain,
was answered, "It is of little use praying for rain so long as the
wind is in the *north !*"—*Local Paper.*

If it rains on a *Sunday before mess,*
It will rain all the week, more or less.

This rule in gardening never forget—
To sow dry and plant wet.

An evening red and a morning grey.
Are sure signs of a fine day.

Friday night's dreams on Saturday told,
Are sure to come true—be they never so old.†

If during the night the temperature fall and the
thermometer rise,
We shall have fine weather and clear skies.

If red the sun begins his race,
Expect that rain will flow apace.

When clouds appear like rocks and towers,
The earth's refreshed with frequent showers.

---

* Mess, *i. e.* mass. Vide *Audelay's Poems*, p. 28, line 10.

† In Sir Thomas Overbury's *Character of a faire and happy Milkmaid*, is the following passage: " Her dreames are so chaste that she dare tell them: only a Fridaie's dreame is all her superstition: that she concealeas for feare of anger." It is unlucky to be bled, take medicine, or get married on a Friday. A child born on a Friday is doomed to misfortune. *Qu.*, Is it unlucky to be buried on a Friday? *Ob.*—That it is *lucky* to be born on a Friday ! and that is just all the luck I ever either heard or read of attending poor Friday.

When the sun sets in a bank,*
A westerly wind we shall not want.

When Roseberry Topping wears a cap,
Let Cleveland then beware of a rap.†

When the wind's in the West,
The weather's always best.

When whins are out of bloom,
Kissing's out of fashion.‡

Easterly winds and rain,
Bring cockles here from Spain.

A man had better ne'er been born,
As have his nails on a Sunday shorn.§

---

* A heavy dark cloud.

† A lofty conical-shaped hill in the North Riding of the county of York. The "rap" alluded to is, in plain language, a thunder-storm. This old proverb is noticed by Camden, two hundred years ago. He observes that, " When its top begins to be darkened with clouds, rain generally follows ;" hence the ancient distich :—

> " When Roseberry Topping weares a cappe,
> Let Clevelande then beware of a clappe."

‡ Whins are *never* out of bloom. The same may be said of groundsel.

§ " To cut nails upon a Friday, or a Sunday, is accounted unlucky amongst the common people in many places. The set and statary times," says Sir Thomas Browne, " of paring nail, and cutting hair, is thought by many a point of consideration.

Cut them on Monday, cut them for health;
Cut them on Tuesday, cut them for wealth.
Cut them on Wednesday, cut them for news;
Cut them on Thursday, for a pair of new shoes.
Cut them on *Friday*, cut them for *sorrow;**
Cut them on Saturday, see your sweetheart to-
morrow.
Cut them on Sunday, cut them for evil;
For all the week long will be with you the *Deevil*.

When Skiddaw hath a cap,
Scruffel wots full well of that.†

He that by the plough would thrive,
Himself must either hold or drive.

The morn to the mountain,
The evening to the fountain.

---

which is perhaps but the continuation of an ancient superstition.
To the Romans it was piacular to pare their nails upon the
nundinæ, observed every ninth day, and was also feared by others
on certain days of the week, according to that of Ausonius,
Ungues Mercurio, barbam Jove, Cypride crines."—*Brand's
Pop. Ant.*, ed. by Sir Hen. Ellis, vol. iii, p. 92.

The Jews, however, (superstitiously, says Mr. Addison, in his
Present State of the Common People, p. 129,) pare their nails on a
Friday.

* The reader will here again observe the "unluckiness" of a
Friday.

† Two lofty mountains on the western borders of England
and Scotland. When Skiddaw "wears" a cloud on its summit
it is ill weather at *Scruffell.* The name of this mountain is properly written Criffell.

Blessed (or happy) is the bride that the sun
shines on:
Blessed (or happy) is the corpse that the rain
rains on.*

There is no gains without pains;
Then plough deep while sluggards sleep.

A quey out of a quey,
Will breed a byre† full of kye.

Drink in the morning staring,
Then all the day be sparing.

An evening red and morning grey,
Is a token of a bonny day.

Early to bed, and early to rise,
Will make a man healthy, wealthy, and wise.

He that will thrive must rise at five;
He who has thriven, may sleep 'till seven.

Plough deep while others sleep,
And you shall have corn to sell and keep.

---

* "If it should happen to rain while the corpse is carried to
church, it is reckoned to bode well to the deceased, whose bier
is wet with the dew of heaven."—*Pennant's Manuscripts.*

"While that others do divine,
Blest is the bride on whom the sun does shine."
—*Herrick's Hesp.*, p. 152.

Byre, byar, or byer. A house in which cows are bound
up. "The mucking of Geordie's byre."—*V. Jam.*

As the days grow longer,
The storms grow stronger.

Some work in the morning may trimly be done,
That all the day after may hardly be won.—

Tusser.

Come day, gang day,
God send Sunday.*

An old moon in a mist,
Is worth gold in a kist (chest);
But a new moon's mist,
Will never lack thirst.†

A northern air,
Brings weather fair.

Monday is Sunday's brother;
Tuesday is such another.
Wednesday you must go to church and pray;
Thursday is half-holiday.
On Friday it is too late to begin to spin;
The Saturday is half-holiday agen.‡

---

* The sluggard's daily prayer.

† *Varia* :—

> As safe as treasure in a kist,
> Is the day in an old moon's mist.

‡ *Divers Crab-tree Lectures,* p. 126. 12mo. Lond. 1639.

If cold wind reach you through a hole,
Say your prayers, and mind your soul.*

The sluggard's guise,
Loth to bed, loth to rise.†

Many haws, many sloes,
Many cold toes.

They that wash on Monday,
  Have a whole week to dry;
They that wash on Tuesday,
  Are not so far agye; (awry)
They that wash on Wednesday,
  May get their clothes clean;
They that wash on Thursday,
  Are not so much to mean;
They that wash on Friday,
  Wash for their need;
But they that wash on Saturdays,
  Are clarty-paps‡ indeed.

---

* A most valuable precept, worthy of all acceptation.
† Nature requires five,
  Custom takes seven,
  Laziness takes nine,
  And Wickedness eleven, } Hours of sleep.
See anecdote of Buffon, *Table Book*, vol. i., col. 796.
‡ Filthy sluts.

When round the moon there is a brugh* [halo],
The weather will be cold and rough.

Wind East or West,
Is a sign of a blast;
Wind North or South,
Is a sign of drought.†

A leap year,
Is never a good sheep year.

When the wind is in the North,
The skilful fisher goes not forth.

To talk of the weather, it's nothing but folly,
For when it rains on the hill, the sun shines in
    the valley.

Where the scythe cuts, and the plough rives,
No more fairies and bee-bikes.‡

When the smoke goes west,
Good weather is past;
When the smoke goes east,
Good weather comes neist [next].

---

* When the halo appears at a distance from the moon, the
storm is supposed to be near at hand. When touching the moon,
the storm is far off.

† To be pronounced "*drouth.*"

‡ This term is still in use for a bee's-nest in a wild state. It
is likewise an archaism. "A byke of waspes bredde in his
nose."—*MS. Cot. Calig.* a. ii., f. 109.

C

When the wind's in the north,
Hail comes forth;
When the wind's in the west,
Look for a wet blast;
When the wind's in the soud [south],
The weather will be fresh and good;
When the wind's in the east,
Cold and snaw comes neist.*

This is silver Saturday,
The morn's the resting day;
On Monday up and to't again,
And Tuesday push away.

The north wind doth blow,
And we shall have snow.

If the cock crows on going to bed,
He's sure to rise with a watery head.†

A Saturday's change brings the boat to the door;
But a Sunday's change brings it upon't mid floor.

When the mist comes from the hill,
Then good weather it doth spill;
When the mist comes from the sea,
Then good weather it will be.

---

* This is the Scots version of the proverb.
† i. e. it will be rain next morning.

The evening grey and morning red,
Make the shepherd hang his head.

When caught by the tempest, wherever it be,
If it lightens and thunders beware of a tree!

For age and want save while you may,
No summer's sun lasts a whole day.

Look to the cow, and the sow, and the wheat mow,
And all will go well enow.

Thirty days hath September,
April, June, and November;
February eight-and-twenty all alone,
And all the rest have thirty-and-one;
Unless that leap-year doth combine,
And give to February twenty-nine.*

The cock does crow,
To let us know,
If we be wise,
'Tis time to rise.

When the clouds are on the hills,
They will come down by the mills.

---

* The above is transcribed from an old book, entitled *The Young Man's Companion*, printed about the year 1703. It likewise appears in an old play, called *The Return from Parnassus*, 4to. Lond.: 1606; and again in Winter's *Cambridge Almanac* for 1635. See *Rara Mathematica*, p. 119.

Time flies awa'
Like snaw in a thaw.

Northerly wind and blubber,
Brings home the Greenland lubber.*

When the sun sets bright and clear,
An easterly wind you need not fear.

When the wind comes before the rain,
You may hoist your topsails up again;
But when the rain comes before the winds,
You may reef when it begins.†

DAYES OF THE WEKE MORALYSED.‡

¶SONDAY.

I am Sonday moste honorable,
  The heed of all yᵉ weke dayes,
That day all thynges laborable
  Ought for to rest and give preyse
To our Creatour, yᵗ alwayes
  Wolde have us reste after trauayle;
Man, seruante, and thy beste, he sayes,
  And yᵉ other to thyne auayle.

---

* A satirical proverb made use of by sailors.
† Although a purely *nautical* proverb, I have nevertheless thought this worthy of insertion.
‡ From an English Primer. Rouen: 1545. Robt. Valentine.

MONDAY.

Monday men ought mee for to call,
　In whiche good workes ought to begynne.
Hearynge masse, ye 1st dede of all;
　Intendynge for to flee dedlye synne,
Thys worldly goodes truely to wynne
　Wyth labor, and true exercyse,
For who of good workes can not blynne
　To his rewarde, shall wynne paradyse.

†TUESDAY.

†I Tuesday am also named of Mars,
　Called of goddes army potent,
I loue neuer for to be scars
　Of workes, but alwayes dylygent,
Striuynge agaynst lyfe indigent,
　Beyng in y^s worlde, or ellse where,
To serue our Lorde with good intent,
　As of duety, we are boonde here.

WEDNESDAY.

†Wenesday, sothely is my name,
　Amydes ye weke is my beynge,
Wherein all vertues dothe frame
　By ye meanes of good lyuynge;
I do remembre ye leuen lykynge
　That was solde in my season;
I do worke with true meanynge,
　Hym for to serue, as it is reason.

†TURSDAY.

†I am y͏ₑ meryest of y͏ᵉ seuen,
  Called tursday, verely;
In my time y͏ᵉ kynge of heuen
  Made his souper merely,
In forme of breade gaue hys body
  To his apostles, as it is playne,
And then washed their fete mekely
  And went to Olyvet mountayne.

†FRIDAY.

†Naamed I am deuoutè fryday,
  The wiche carethe for no delyte,
But to mourne, faste, deale, and pray;
  I do set all my hole apetyte
To thykne on y͏ᵉ Jewes despyte,
  Howe they dyd Chryste on y͏ᵉ rent;
And thynkynge howe I may be quyte
  At y͏ᵉ dredefull judgement.

†SATERDAY.

†Saterday I am comeyng laste,
  Trustynge on y͏ᵉ tyme wel spente,
Hauyng euer mynde stedfaste
  On that lorde y͏ᵗ harowed hell,
That my synnes wyll expall,
  At y͏ᵉ instaunce of his mother,
Whose goodnesse dothe farre excell
  Whome I serue aboue all other.
              Amen.

JANUARY.

A good new year, and a merry Handsel Monday.*

Janiveer freeze the pot by the fire.

January never lies dead in a dyke gutter.

March in January, January in March I fear.

Winter never rots in the sky.

On St. Distaff's day—neither work nor play.†

Praise we the Lord that hath no peer,
And thank we Him for this new year.

If new-year's eve night-wind blow *South*,
It betokeneth warmth and growth;
If *West*, much milk, and fish in the sea;
If *North*, much cold, and storms there will be;
If *East*, the trees will bear much fruit,—
If north-east, flee it man and brute.

At new-year's tide,
The days lengthen a cock's stride.‡

---

* Hansel Monday is the first Monday in the new year.

† January 7th : called by country people, St. Distaff's Day, or Rock Day, because (the Christmas holidays having ended) good housewives resumed in part, but not in whole, the distaff and their other industrious avocations.

‡ This saying is intended to express the lengthening of the days in a small, but perceptible degree. The countryman well knows the truth of what he says, from observing where the shadow of the upper lintel of his door falls at twelve o'clock,

Many hips and haws,
Many frosts and snaws.

If the grass grows in Janiveer,
It grows the worse for't all the year.

Remember on St. Vincent's day*
If the sun his beams display,
Be sure to mark the transient beam
Which through the casement sheds a gleam;
For 'tis a token bright and clear,
Of prosperous weather all the year.

If St. Paul's day† be fair and clear,
It doth betide a happy year;

---

and there making a mark. At new year's day, the sun at the
meridian being higher, its shadow comes nearer the door by
four or five inches, which for rhyme's sake is called a "cock's
stride;" and so expresses the sensible increase of the day.—
Gent. Mag. 1759.

   * January 22. The Germans have a proverb:—

> "Um Vinzenzen Sonnenschein,
> Füllt die Fässer mit korn und wein."

The French have many proverbs relating to St. Vincent's day.

   † Jan. 25. The Germans have a proverb:—

> "Sanct Paulus klar,
> Bringt gutes Jahr;
> So er bringt wind,
> Regnet's geschwind."

The French verses on this day resemble closely the English ones
given above:—

> "De Saint Paul la claire journée
> Nous denote une bonne année;
> S'il fait vent nous aurons la guerre,
> S'il neige ou pleut cherté sur terre;
> S'on voit fort espois les brouillards,
> Mortalité de toutes parts."

But if by chance it then should rain,*
It will make dear all kinds of grain;
And if the clouds make dark the sky,
Then neat† and fowls this year shall die;
If blustering winds do blow aloft,
Then wars shall trouble the realm full oft.

New moon, new moon, I hail thee!
By all the virtue in my body,
Grant this night that I may see,
He who my true love is to be.‡

A January haddock,
A February bannock,
And a March pint of ale.‖

A January spring
Is worth naething.

---

* *Varia.* "But if it chance to snow and rain." The festival
of the Conversion of St. Paul has always been reckoned ominous
of the future weather of the year, in various countries remote
from each other.

† Cattle.

‡ This verse is repeated by country maidens at the first
appearance of the new moon next after New Year's Day,—though
some are so *ignorant* as to say that any other new moon is
equally as good, — in order that they may see their future
husbands.

‖ Are to be preferred before those of any other month.

. Under water dearth,
Under snow bread.

As the day lengthens,
So the cold strengthens.*

Who in January sows oats, gets gold and groats;
Who sows in May, gets little that way.

If January calends be summerly gay,
'Twill be winterly weather till the calends of May.

If you but knew how good it were,
To eat a pullet in Janiveer,
If you had twenty in your flock,
You'd leave but one to go with the cock.

The blackest month in all the year,
Is the month of Janiveer.

FEBRUARY.

Of all the months in the year, curse a fair February.
On Candlemas-day,—good goose lay!
On Candlemas-day, throw cards and candlesticks away.†

---

* This proverb sometimes appears under the form,—

When the days lengthen,
The frost is sure to strengthen.

† It is to be noted, that from Candlemas the use of tapers at vespers and litanies, which prevailed throughout the winter, ceased until the ensuing All Hallow Mass, and hence the origin of this time-worn English proverb. Candlemas candle-

A windy Christmas and a calm Candlemas, are signs
of a good year.

If Candlemas-day be fine, it portends a hard season to
come ;

If Candlemas-day be cloudy and lowering, a mild and
gentle season.

Fit as a pan-cake for Shrove Tuesday.*

Coupled like birds on St. Valentine's day.

Sow or set beans on Candlemas waddle.†

St. Matthew [24 Feb.] breaks the ice; if he finds none
he will make it.‡

Februeer doth cut and shear.

February builds a bridge, and March breaks it down.

My Candlemas bond upon you.§

As long as the bird sings before Candlemas, it will
greet after it.

As big as bull beef at Candlemas.

---

carrying remained in England till its abolition by an order in
council, in the second year of K. Edw. VI.

 * The pancake was anciently a universal dish on this festival;
I myself have many times and oft partaken of them. Shrove
Tuesday in the north of England is generally called Pancake
Tuesday. A dish of fritters at supper is usual in France on
this day and the following Thursday. See Hone's *Year Book*,
146-7-8 and 9. In Lancashire hot pancakes are to this day *intro-
duced* at the tea table on Shrove Tuesday.

 † In Somersetshire, "waddle" means the wane of the moon.

 ‡ A German proverb:—

    Matheis bricht's eis,
    Find't er keins, so macht er eins.

 § See *Every Day Book*, vol. i. col. 12.

February is seldom warm.*
Never clean your nails on Candlemas-day.

The hind† had as lief see his wife on the bier,
As that Candlemas day be pleasant and clear.

If Candlemas-day be fair and bright,
Winter will have another flight.

If Candlemas-day is fair and clear,
There'll be two winters in the year.‡

If Candlemas-day be clouds and rain,
Winter is gone, and will not come again.

---

* " Soulegrove sil lew," is an ancient Wiltshire proverb.
† A married agricultural servant.
‡ In the old French *Calendrier des bons Laboureurs*, we are
told,—
> " Selon les anciens le dit,
> Si le soleil clair luit
> A la chandeleur, vous croirez
> Qu'encor un hyuer vous aurez."

The Germans have a similar saying. A correspondent to
Hone's *Year Book*, p. 140, says: "I have seen a farmer of the
' Old School,' rubbing his hands with glee during the dismal
battling of the elements without, while the wind entered within
through the crevices of the doors and casements of the latticed
windows, while his children, at the loud blasts that roared round
the roof, ran for protection between the knees of their father, or
hid their faces in the lap of their mother. When the young ones
were put to bed, the two old folks would sit on the side of the
ingle neuk, talking ' o' th' days o' langsine,' when they were
bairns themselves, and confirming each other in the belief of the

When Candlemas day is come and gone,
The snow lies on a hot stone.

February fill-dike, be it black or be it white,
But if it be white, it's the better to like.

If Candlemas-day be dry and fair,
The half of winter's to come and mair [more].

If Candlemas-day be wet and foul,
The half of winter's gone at Yule.*

February, if ye be fair,
The sheep will mend, and nothing mair;
February, if ye be foul,†
The sheep will die in every pool.

---

old prognostication." Bishop Hall, in a sermon on this day,
remarks, that "it hath been an old (I say not how true) note,
that hath been wont to be set on this day, that if it be clear and
sun-shiny, it portends a hard winter to come; if cloudy and
louring, a mild and gentle season ensuing." Browne, in his
Vulgar Errors, says, that "there is a general tradition in most
parts of Europe that inferreth the coldness of the succeeding
winter from the shining of the sun on Candlemas-day, according
to the proverbial distich:—

"Si sol splendescat Maria purificante,
Major erit glacies post festum quam fuit ante."

The Germans say, "The badger peeps out of his hole on
Candlemas-day, and if he finds snow he walks abroad; if he
sees the sun shining, he draws back again into his hole." The
French have a similar saying of the bear.

* Christmas.
† *i. e.* rainy, not snowy.

First comes Candlemas, then the new moon,
And the next Tuesday after is Fasten's e'en,*

On Candlemas-day, you must hae
Half your straw, and half your hay.

At new-year's day, a cock's stride,
At Candlemas, an hour wide.†

Collop Monday, pancake Tuesday,
Ash Wednesday, bloody Thursday;
Friday's lang, but will be *dune*,
And hey for Saturday afternune!‡

Now§ end the whiteloafe and the pye,
And let all sports with Christmas dye.¶

In February, if thou hearst thunder,
Thou wilt see a summer's wonder.

---

* See Chambers's *Pop. Rhy. Scott.* ed. 1842, p. 38.

† Said in allusion to the lengthening of the day.

‡ This is a Shrove-tide rhyme; and, I believe, peculiar to the north of England. The Rev. Mr. Bowles communicates to his friend, Mr. Brand, that the boys in the neighbourhood of Salisbury go about before Shrove-tide, singing these lines:—

> Shrove-tide is nigh at hand,
> And I am come a shroving;
> Pray, dame, something,
> An apple, or a dumpling;
> Or a piece of truckle-cheese,
> Of your own making;
> Or a piece of pancake.

§ Candlemas eve.

¶ From Herrick.

On Candlemas-day, a good goose will lay;
But on Valentine's day, any goose will lay.

The Welchman would rather see his dam on her
  bier,
Than see a fair Februeer.

February fills the dyke,
Either with black or white.*

MARCH.

March comes in like a lion, and goes out like a lamb.
A peck of March dust is worth a king's ransom.
A dry March never begs its bread.
March grass never did good.
The spring is not always green.†
Sow wheat in dirt and rye in dust.
One swallow does not make a spring, nor a woodcock
  a winter.
A windy March and a showery April make a beautiful
  May.
A March wisher, is never a good fisher.
March birds are best.
Mad as a March hare.‡

---

* *e. i.* either with rain or snow.

† March 6th, spring quarter commences. Some writers date
from the 20th.

‡ See Halliwell's *Introduction to "A Midsummer Night's Dream,"*
p. 2 and 3; and his *Archaic Dict.*, vol. ii., art. "March-hare."

Lent seems short to him that borrows money to be
   paid at Easter.

March comes in with an adder's head, and goes out
   with a peacock's tail.

March many weathers.

A wet spring is a sign of dry weather for harvest.

As hard as an egg at Easter.

I'll warrant you for an egg at Easter, [*i. e.*, be bound
   for you].*

So many frosts in March, so many in May.

Black lad Monday.†

As bashful as a Lentel lover.‡

---

* Paste or Pace, whether applied to the season or an egg, is
unquestionably a corruption of Pasche, or Pasque; which latter
terms, I judge, are derived from the Jewish festival of the pass-
over, or pascal supper, answering to the Pagan-Saxon feast of
the goddess Eoster, and the Christian celebration of our
Saviour's resurrection.

   The egg simply signifies, or is, a fit emblem of the resurrection of Christ, and of ours though him to everlasting life.

   The customary egg-feast, though varying greatly in every
country both in form and fashion, is retained to the present day
by Pagan and Jew; as well as by those of the Mahomedan,
Romish, Greek, Scottish, and Anglican churches: and though,
perhaps, foolish to an extreme,—according to the form prac-
tised in England, it has this good property, it is an innocent
one !

   † The Monday in Easter-week.

   ‡ A Lentel lover is one who is afraid to touch his mistress.—
Cotgrave, in v. Caresme.

He that hath not a palm in his hand on **Palm** Sunday
must have his hand cut off.*

If the sun shines on Easter-day, it shines on Whit-
Sunday likewise.†

Sow thin, shear thin.

---

* Though Roman Catholic customs were generally disused
under Henry VIII, yet he declared that the bearing of palms on
Palm Sunday was to be continued and not cast away. It appears
they were borne in England till the 2nd of Edward VI. In
Stowe's *Chronicle*, by Howes, the practice is said to have been
discontinued in 1548.—*Brand.*

Naorgeorgus, translated by Barnaby Googe, says:—

> "The people all do come, and bowes of trees and palmes they beare,
> Which things against y° tempest great, y° parson conjures there."

Again:—

> "The shaven priests before them marche, y° people follow fast,
> Still striving who shall gather first y° bowes y* downe are cast,
> For falsely they believe y* these have force and virtue greate,
> Against y° rage of winter stormes and thunder's flashing heate."

Again:—

> "Besides they candles up do light, of virtue like in all,
> And willow-branches hallow, y they palmes do use to call;
> This done, they verily believe y° tempest nor ye storm,
> Can neyther hurts themselves, nor yet y° cattel, nor y° corne."

The willow in England is a tree of quick growth; it is a common observation "That the willow will buy a horse, before the
oak will pay for a *saddle*." The palm willow, with its velvet-
looking buds, are occasionally still stuck in some village churches
on Palm Sunday.

† *Countryman's Counsellor*, Lond. 1633, p. 220.

Upon St. David's day,
Put oats and barley in the clay.

First comes David,* next comes Chad,†
And then comes Winnold,‡ as though he was mad.

An ague in the spring,
Is physic for a king.§

Tid, mid, and misera,
Carling, palm, and paste-egg day.‖

---

* 1st March.   † 2nd March.

‡ A corruption of *Winwaloe*; Father Porter calls him *Winwa-loke*, and Father Cressy, *Winwaloc*. This proverb alludes to the windy weather which prevails at this period of the year; but whether Winnold, when in the zenith of his power and fame, was remarkable for an irascibility of temper, I really do not know. His day is the 3rd of March.

§ This reminds me of the following charm for the ague, which should be repeated by the most ancient female in the family or neighbourhood, with her head as far up the *chimney* as conveniently it can be got, viz. :—

Tremble and go!
First day, shiver and burn ;
Tremble and quake!
Second day, shiver and learn,
Tremble and die!
Third day, never return.

‖ Easter day. The first line of this "old saw" is evidently a corruption of the Psalms, according to the Latin translation, beginning *Te Deum, Mi Deus*, and *Miserere mei.*

Varia :—

Tid, mid, et misera,
Carling, Palm, and good Pace-day.

Care Sunday, care away,
Palm-Sunday and Easter-day.

According to the number of magpies you see at one
and the same time when going a journey, &c., you
may calculate your luck as follows:—

One for sorrow,
Two for luck (*varia.* mirth);
Three for a wedding,
Four for death (*varia.* birth);
Five for silver,
Six for gold;
Seven for a secret,
Not to be told;
Eight for heaven,
Nine for ——,
And ten *for the d——l's own sell!*

The following is a common address to the magpie
in the whole of the north of England:—

Magpie, magpie, chatter and flee,
Turn up thy tail, and good luck fall me!

In March, kill crow, pie,* and cadow,†
Rook, buzzark, and raven;
Or else go desire them
To seek a new haven.

---

* Magpie.　　　† Jackdaw.

March winds and April showers,
Bring forth May flowers.*

A bushel of March dust is a thing,
Worth the ransom of a king.†

So many mists in March you see,
So many frosts in May will be.

When Easter falls in our lady's lap,
Then let England beware of a rap.‡

When the sloe-tree is white as a sheet,
Sow your barley whether it be dry or wet.

---

* So the Germans say,—

> "Märzen wind und Aprilen regen,
> Verheissen im Mai grossen segen."

And the French:—

> "Mars venteux, Avril pluvieux,
> Font le Mai gai et gracieux."

† A dry March makes the clay lands of England bear abundant crops of corn; consequently, if in this month the weather is such as to make the highways dusty, the country will be benefited to the amount of a "king's ransom." In German there is a similar saying: "Ein loth Märzen staub ist einen ducaten werth,"—half-an-ounce of March dust is worth a ducat.

‡ Meaning thereby, that when the festival of Easter falls near to Lady-day (the 25th March), England is threatened with some calamity,

March *borrowit* from April,
Three days and they were ill:
The first was frost,
The second was *snaw*;
And the third as *cauld*,
As ever't could *blaw*.*

---

* These days being generally stormy, our forefathers have
endeavoured to account for this circumstance by pretending that
March *borrowed* them from April, that he might extend his
powers so much longer.   Those who are addicted to superstition
will neither borrow nor lend on any of these days.—*Dr. Jamie-
son's Etymo. Dict.*

> "March said to Aperill
> I see three hogs upon a hill;
> But lend your three first days to me,
> And I'll be bound to gar them die.
> The first, it sall be wind and weet;
> The next, it sall be snaw and sleet,
> The third, it sall be sic a freeze
> Shall gar the birds stick to the trees.
> But when the borrowed days were gane,
> The three silly hogs cam hirplin hame."
>
> *The Complaynt of Scotland, 8vo. Edinb. 1801.*

In the *B-itish Apollo*, vol. iii., no. 18, the meaning is asked of
the old saying:—

> "March borrows from April
> Three days, and they are ill;
> April returns them back again,
> Three days and they are rain."

"*Ans.* Proverbs relating to the weather cannot be founded on
any certainty. The meaning of this is that it is more seasonable
for the end of March and the beginning of April to be fair, but
often,—

> "March does from April gain
> Three days, and they're in rain;
> Return'd by April in's bad kind,
> Three days, and they're in wind."

[Old

The cuckoo comes of mid March,
And cucks of mid Aperill;
And gauns away of Midsummer month,
When the corn begins to fill.*

If they would drink nettles in March,
And eat mugwort in May,

Old farmers in Devonshire call the three first days of March "blind days"; and they were anciently considered so unlucky that no husbandman would sow any seed on any of the three. This singular old proverb in Ray's Collection reads thus: "April borrows three days from March, and they are ill." So says Brand.

"The *Favilteach*, or three first days of *February*, serve many poetical purposes in the Highlands. They are said to have been borrowed from January, who was bribed by February with three young sheep. These three days, by Highland reckoning, occur between the 11th and 15th of February; and it is accounted a most favourable prognostic for the ensuing year that they be as stormy as possible. If they should be fair, then there is no more good weather to be expected through the spring."—*Mrs. Grant's Superstitions of the Highlanders*, vol. ii., p. 217.

* "If you have money in your pockets," say the Germans, "when the cuckoo first cries, all will go well during the year; and if you were fasting, you would be hungry the whole year."—*Grimm's Deutsche Mythologie.*

Perhaps the following local rhyme may not be unacceptable:—

The cuckoo's a bonny bird,
He whistles as he flies;
He brings us good tidings,
He tells us no lies.
He sucks little birds' eggs,
To make his throat clear;
And never sings cuckoo,
Till the spring time of year.

So many fine maidens,
Wouldn't go to the clay.*

On the first of March,
The crows begin to search.†

March dust and May sun,
Makes corn white and maids dun.

March wind and May sun,
Makes clothes clear and maidens dun.

March wind,
Kindles‡ the ether,§ and blooms the whin.‖

A late spring,
Is a great bless-ing.¶

---

* This is a piece of Scottish superstition; and if I am informed truly, there is, in connexion with it, either a fairy or witchcraft story.

† Crows are supposed to commence pairing on this day.

‡ Enlivens.

§ Adder.

‖ *Varia:*—

> March wind,
> Wakens the ether, and blooms the thorn.

Shakspeare thus notices this vernal proverb,—

> " It is the bright day that brings forth the adder,
> And that craves wary walking."
>
> *Julius Cæsar,* act ii. sc. 1.

¶ Better late ripe and bear, than early blossom and blast.

Sow peas and beans on David and Chad,
Be the weather good or bad.

Sow beans in the mud,
And they'll grow like a wood.

One a penny buns, two a penny buns,
One a penny, two a penny, hot cross buns,
Butter them, and sugar them, and put them in
your *muns.**

On or before St. Chad,†
Every goose lays—both good and bad.

———

APRIL.

One swallow does not make a summer.‡
April and May are the keys of the whole year.
A·cold April, the barn will fill.

———

* This rhyme is occasionally still repeated in the north of England. It is peculiar to Good-Friday.
† March 2nd.
‡ The 15th of April is, in some parts of England, known by the name of "swallow-day." Willsford, in his *Nature's Secrets*, p. 134, says, "Swallows flying low, and touching ye water often with yr wings, presage rain."

The cuckoo has picked up the dirt.*
April with fools, and May with bastards blest.†

On the first of April,
Hunt the gowke another mile.‡

An April shower and May sun,
Will make cloth white, and fair maids dun.

April with his hack and his bill,
Plants a flower on every hill.

On the third of April,
Comes in the cuckoo and nightingale.§

When April blows his horn,‖
It's good for both hay and corn.

---

* Said in allusion to the dry weather at this period of the year. The 14th April is in Sussex called "first cuckoo day."

† From Churchill.

‡ In Westmorland and Cumberland, an April fool is termed an *April gowk*, one that is the bearer of a fool's errand. Brand says, "that *gowk* is properly a *cuckoo*, and is used here metaphorically for a fool; this is correct, for from the Saxon *gaec*, a cuckoo, is derived *geck*, which means 'one easily imposed on.'"

§ The 14th April is in Sussex called "first cuckoo day."

‖ *i. e.* when in this month winds prevail, it is good for both meadow and tillage lands. The Germans have precisely the same proverb:—

> Wenn April bläst in sein horn,
> So steht es gut um heu und kern.

When the cuckoo comes to the bare thorn,
Sell your cow, and buy your corn ;
But when she comes to the full bit,
Sell your corn, and buy your sheep.

In April, the cuckoo shews his bill;
In May, he sings both night and day;
In June, he altereth his tune ;
In July, away he'll fly;
In August, go he must.*

Sow peas and beans in the wane of the moon,
Who soweth them sooner, he soweth too soon.†

April showers
Bring May flowers.

It was at no very distant period a custom, even with people of
fashion, to wear a *blue coat* on the 23rd of April, in honour of
St. George.

"To hang an egg laid on Ascension day in the roof of an
house, preserveth it from all hurts."—*Scott's Discovery of Witchcraft*, p. 152,

* See a various version in Halliwell's *Nursery Rhymes of
England*, 4th ed. p. 165. See Wright's *Selection of Latin Stories*,
printed for the Percy Society, pp. 42, 74, 224.

† That they, with ye planet, may rest and rise,
And flourish with bearing most plentiful wise.—*Tusser.*

"Peas and beans, sown during the increase, do run more to
hawm and straw; and during ye declension, more to cod, according to the common consent of countrymen."—*Tusser Redivivus.*
8vo. Lond. 1744, p. 16.

An April flood,
Carries away the frog and his brood.

An April cling,
Is good for nothing.*

When Luna lowres,
Then April showres.†

MAY.

As fine as a May-pole on May-day.‡
As welcome as flowers in May.
A hot May makes a fat church-yard.
Cast not a clout—'till May be out.§
May rain kills lice.‖
A May flood—never did good.
You must look for grass on the top of the oak tree.
The merry month of May.
He'll never climb May-hill; or,
If he can climb over May-hill he'll do.¶

---

* A Somersetshire proverb.

† *Travels of Two-Pence*, 1620.

‡ This evidently refers to the custom of decking the may-pole, on May-day, with ribbons and garlands.

§ The great prevalence of easterly winds during this month, appears to me the chief cause of this well-known injunction.

‖ I never either heard or saw an explanation of this *rather* coarse proverb.

¶ Dr. Forster, in his *Perennial Calendar*, has a note on these two sayings. *Note.*—May is considered a *trying month* for health.

As sweet as lilies in May.
As white as a lily in May.
"As mery as flowres in May."*

He that would live for aye,
Must eat sage in May.

A wet May,
Will fill a byre full of hay.

May-day is come and gone,
Thou art a gosling and I am none.†

A cold May, and a windy,
Makes a fat (full) barn and a findy.‡

---

* *MS. Cantab.* ff. v. 48. p. 111.

† A May-gosling (provincially, *gesling*), on the first of May, is made with as much eagerness in the county of Westmorland, and other parts of the north of England, as an April noddy, noodle, fool, or gowk, on the 1st of April. See *Gent.'s Mag.*, for April, 1791. And should an attempt be made to make any one a May-gosling on the 2nd of May, this rhyming saying is retorted upon them.

This distich was also said, *mutatis mutandis*, on the 2nd of April.

‡ Several proverbs to the same effect are found in German ; one is,—
> Kühler Mai
> Giebt guten wein und vieles heu.

He who bathes in May,
Will soon be laid in clay;*
He who bathes in June,
Will sing a merry tune;
He who bathes in July,
Will dance like a fly.

A swarm of bees in May,†
Is worth a load of hay;

---

* The present month (May) being one when very severe colds
are often caught by others as well as bathers, it may not be
amiss to submit this portion, particularly, to the serious consideration of my readers. This old saying is very rife in some
districts in Yorkshire, Craven especially.

† In Tusser's *Five Hundred Points of Husbandry*, are these lines,
under May:—

> "Take heed to y^r bees, y^t are ready to swarme,
> The losse y^{re} of now is a crown's worth of harme."

A Warwickshire correspondent in Hone's *Every-day Book*,
vol. i., col. 647, says, that in that county, "The first swarm of
bees is simply called a ' swarm;' the second from the same hive
is called a ' cast;' and the third from the same hive a 'spindle.'"

Willsford, in his *Nature's Secrets*, p. 134, says, "Bees, in fair
weather, not wandering far from y^r hives, presages ye approach
of some stormy weather."

When you purchase a hive of bees, you should not pay for
them in money, but in goods; for instance, if you are a farmer,
give an equivalent in wheat, oats, or barley, &c., and never
presume to bring them home till the *Good-Friday* following.
Apiarians would do well to follow this wholesome piece of
advice.

[The

A swarm of bees in June,
Is worth a silver *spune* ;*
A swarm of bees in July,
Is not worth a fly !†

If you look at your corn in May,
You'll come weeping away;
If you look at the same in June,
You'll come home in another tune.

When the oak puts oh his gosling gray,
'Tis time to sow barley, night and day.‡

The proverb is also found in German :—

> Ein bienenschwarm im Mai
> Ist werth ein fuder heu ;
> Aber ein schwarm im Juni
> Der lohnet kaum die müh.

The day of the week on which the 14th of May fell, used, some sixty or seventy years ago (so I have heard my seniors say), to be considered an unlucky day; no one ever beginning business of any serious moment upon it for the rest of the year.

* *Varia.*—Is only or not worth a crown.

† This is quoted in Miege's *Great French Dictionary*, fol. Lond. 1687, second part.

‡ When the oak puts out its leaf before the ash, a dry summer may be expected. When the ash puts out its leaf before the oak, a wet and cold one. An observation pretty well founded on experience.

A superstitious notion once prevailed in England, "that

When the elder is white, brew and bake a peck;
When the elder is black, brew and bake a sack.

Mist in May, and heat in June,
Makes the harvest right soon.*

He who sows oats in May,
Gets little that way.†

The first of May
Is Robin Hood's day.‡

---

whatsoever one did ask of God upon Whitsunday morning, at the instant when the sun rose, and played, God would grant it him." See Arise Evans's *Echo of the Voice of Heaven*; or a *Narration of his Life*, 8vo. Lond. 1652, p. 9. He says, " he went up a hill to see y⁰ sun rise betimes on Whitsunday morning," and saw it at its rising, "skip, play, dance, and turn about like a wheel."

Camden, in his *Ancient and Modern Manners of the Irish*, says, "They fancy a green bough of a tree, fastened on May-day against a house, will produce plenty of milk that summer."

In the *Survey of the South of Ireland*, p. 233, we read, "The sun was propitiated here by sacrifices of fire; one was on the 1st of May, for a blessing on the seed sown."

* In Scotland, they say,—

> A wet May and a winnie,
> Brings a fou stackyard and a finnie.

† *i. e.* he will be sure to reap a bad and unproductive crop.

‡ See Strutt's *Sports and Pastimes*, Hone's edition, p. 354.

Twenty-ninth of May,
Royal-oak day.*

May, come she early, or come she late,
She'll make the cow to quake.

Beans blow,
Before May doth grow.

From the marriages in May,
All the bairns die and decay.†

———

JUNE.

A dry summer ne'er made a dear peck.‡
An English summer—two fine days and a thunder-
storm.
There's no summer, but it has a winter.

———

* *Varia.*—Oaken-apple day.

† See Hone's *Year-Book*, col. 76. " May birds are aye cheep-
ing."—*Pop. Rhy. Scotland*, p. 74. An old poet sings:—

> " May never was ye month of love,
> For May is full of flowers;
> But rather April wet by kind,
> For love is full of showers."

Even as far back as the days of Ovid, it was considered a bad
omen to be married in May.

‡ Summer quarter commences 21st June.

May and June are twin sisters.*
A good hay year—a bad fog year.
The sun shines on both sides of the hedge.†
Welcome as snow in summer, and rain in harvest.

———

If St. Vitus's day‡ be rainy weather,
It will rain for thirty days together.

He who marries between the syckle and the scythe,
Will never thrive.§

Calm weather in June,
Sets corn in tune.

———

* I believe that June is represented under the type of a young man; consequently, this proverbial phrase appears rather paradoxical.

† Said of summer, when the sun ascends so high in the heavens that the shadow of hedges is scarcely perceptible. In England, no absolute darkness takes place between the 23rd May and 20th July.

‡ June 15th. This proverb is applied by the French and Germans to the day of St. Medard, and sometimes to that of St. Gervase, both in June.

§ The inferences to be drawn from this proverb are not to be contemned by farmers and husbandmen; but should they be so wilful as to do so, they may, it is possible, ere the termination of the year, or the rent-day approach, find a little leisure time in which to rue. Perhaps this proverb was more strictly true when our forefathers devoted a whole month in which to celebrate their nuptials, to the great neglect of all other matters.

E

Barnaby bright,
The longest day
And shortest night.*

A good leak in June,
Sets all in tune.

When the fern is as high as a spoon,
You may sleep an hour at noon.

If woolly fleeces spread the heavenly way,
No rain, be sure, disturbs the summer's day.

JULY.

. St. Swithin is christening the apples.†
All shearers are honest in the harvest field.‡
A bad shearer never had a good syckle.

---

* This Barnaby-day, or thereabout, is the summer solstice, or sun-sted, when the sun seems to stand, and begins to go back, being the longest day in the yeare, about the 11th (St. Barnabas day) or 12th of June; it is taken for the whole time, when the dayes appear not for xiv days together, either to lengthen or shorten.—*Festa Anglo-Romana*, p. 72.

† A common observation on this (St. Swithin's) day, should it chance to be a rainy one.

‡ So honest as never to be known to cut a single stem belonging to their neighbour's " rig."

A green shear is an ill shake.

As bright as the sun on a summer's day.

It is midsummer's noon with you.*

Welcome as rain at harvest.

Make your hay while the sun shines.†

If deer rise up dry and lie down dry on St. (Martin) Bullion's day,‡ it is a sign there will be a good gose harvest.

In July, shear your rye.

Whoever eats oysters on St. James's day will never want money.§

---

* *i. e.* you are gone "clean mad."

† Duncomb's answer in hay-time, relating to the weather:—

> "Well, Duncomb, how will be the weather?
> Sir, it looks cloudy altogether.
> And coming 'cross our Haughton Green,
> I stopp'd and talk'd with old Frank Beane;
> While we stood there, sir, old Jan Swain,
> Went by and said, he know'd 'twould rain.
> The next that came was Master Hunt,
> And he declar'd he knew it wont.
> And then I met with Farmer Blow,
> He plainly told me he didn't know:
> So, sir, when doctors disagree,
> Who's to decide it, you or me?"

Duncomb was an original and a rhymer. His occupation was that of dealer in Dunstable larks. He resided for many years at the village of Haughton-Regis, near Dunstable.

‡ St. Bullion's day is the 4th July. This is a Scots proverb.

§ On this day (25th July, O. S.), in London, oysters come in season. The indifference to industry which such notions may possibly engender in many minds, can, it is more than probable, be testified by some, who themselves falsify the legend by their present abode in prisons or in workhouses.

If it rains on Midsummer eve, all the filberts will be
spoiled.

———

If the first of July be rainy weather,
'Twill rain *mair* or less for forty days togéther.*

A cherry year—a merry year :
A plum year—a dumb year.

The first cock of hay
Frights the cuckoo away.

In July, some reap rye;
In August, if one will not, the other must.

St. Swithin's day, if thou dost rain,
For forty days it will remain :
St. Swithin's day, if thou be fair,
For forty days 'twill rain *na mair.*†

———

* This saying is applied in German to several days in the
month of July.

† The frivolous monkish legend of St. Swithin causing the
ráin to fall so copiously from heaven as to prevent the removal
of his bones from the cemetery-garth to within the precincts of
the minster church of Winchester, in the year 685, is too com-
mon-place to deserve notice here. Those who are unacquainted
with the fable, will find it duly and *truly* recorded in Hone's
Every-day Book, vol. i. col. 954.

[In

No tempest, good July,
Lest corn come off blue by.

In *Poor Robin's Almanack* for 1697, the prognostic is thus
recorded:—

> "In this month is St. Swithin's day;
> On which, if that it rain, they say,
> Full xl days after it will,
> Or more or less some rain distill.
> This Swithin was a saint, I trow,
> And Winchester's bp. also,
> Who in his time did many a feat,
> As popish legends do repeat."

Gay, in his *Trivia*, writes:—

> "How if, on Swithin's feast the welkin lours,
> And ev'ry pent-house streams with hasty show'rs,
> Twice twenty days shall clouds their fleeces drain,
> And wash the pavements with incessant rain."

Churchill thus glances at the superstitious notions about rain
on St. Swithin's day:—

> "July to whom the dog-star in her train,
> St. James gives oysters, and St. Swithin rain." -

In Mr. Howard's work on the Climate of London, cited by
Dr. Forster, in his *Per. Calendar*, is the following remark:—
"To do justice to popular observation, I may now state, that in
a majority of our summers, a showery period, which, with some
latitude as to time and local circumstances, may be admitted to
constitute daily rain for xl days, does come on about the time
indicated by this tradition : not that any long space before is
often so dry as to mark distinctly its commencement."

' *Query.*—May not the foolish and superstitious idea of xl days'
rain after St. Swithin, have originated in a still more ancient
tradition of Noah having on that day entered the ark ? " when
the foundations of the great deep were broken up, and the
windows of heaven were opened, and it rained for xl days and

Till St. James's day* be come and gone,
You may have hops, or you may have none.

Bow-wow, dandy fly,
Brew no beer in July.

Many rains, many rowans ;
Many rowans,† many yawns.‡

AUGUST.

Short harvests, make short *addlings*.
Good harvests make men prodigal; bad ones, provident.

---

nights," so that the highest hills under heaven were covered with the waters.

July 3rd, the dog-days begin. Our forefathers supposed that the malignant influence of the dog-star, when in conjunction with the sun, caused the sea to boil, wine to become sour, dogs to go mad, and all other creatures to languish; while in men it produced increase of bile, hysterics, phrensies, burning fevers, and other malignant disorders! They likewise had an opinion, that during those days all physic should be declined, and the cure committed to nature: this season is called the *Physician's vacation*.

* July 25th.
† Rowans are the fruit of the mountain-ash; and an abundance thereof is held to denote a deficient harvest.
‡ Light grains of wheat, oats, or barley.

A good nut year—a good corn year.*

A long harvest leaves little corn.

At latter Lammas.†

At St. Barthol'mew,‡

Then comes cold dew.

SEPTEMBER.

He, who would reap well, must sow well.

---

* Willsford, in his *Nature's Secrets*, p. 144, informs us that,
"In autumn (some say), in the *gall*, or oak-apple, one of these
iii things will be found (if cut in pieces) : a flie, denoting *want*;
a worm, *plenty*; but if a spider, mortality." Again, he says,
ibid., that "the *broom*, having plenty of blossoms, or the *walnut*
tree, is a sign of a fruitful year of corn." That "great store of
nuts and *amonds* presage a plentiful year of corn, especially
filberds."

Lupton, in his third *Book of Notable Things* (edit. 8vo., 1660,
p. 52), No. 7, says: "If you take an *oak-apple* from an oak tree,
and open the same, you shall find a little worm therein, which if
it doth creep, it betokens scarceness of corn. This is the
countryman's astrology, which they have long observed for
truth."

† Synonymous with the *Ad Græcas Calendas* of the Latins;
and the vulgar saying, "When two Sundays come together,"
i. e. never. "It happened in the reign of Queen Dick," is
another proverb of the same class.

‡ August 24.

If you eat goose on St. Michael's day,* you will never
want money all the year.†

So many days old the moon is on Michaelmas-day, so
many floods after.‡

---

* Or Michaelmas day, 29th September.

† See note on oyster-eating on St. James's day, in Proverbs
for July. In the *British Apollo*, fol. Lond. 1708, vol. i, no. 74,
is the following:—

Qu. " ——— ——— ——— Pray tell me whence
The custom'd proverb did commence,
That who eats *goose* on Michael's-day,
Sha'nt money lack, his debts to pay.

An. This notion, fram'd in days of yore,
Is grounden on a prudent score;
For, doubtless, 'twas at first design'd,
To make the people *seasons* mind;
That so they may apply their care,
To all those things which needful were,
And by a good industrious hand,
Know *when* and *how* t'improve their land."

In the x year of King Edward IV, John de la Hay was bound,
among other services, to render to Will. Barnaby, lord of Lastres,
in the county of Hereford, for a parcel of demesne lands, one
goose, fit for the lord's dinner, on the feast of St. Michael the
Archangel.—*Blount's Tenures, Beckwith's edit.*, p. 222.

We have the authority of Mr. Douce for saying, "that Queen
Elizabeth received the news of the defeat of the Spanish Armada
whilst she was eating a *goose* on Michaelmas day.

Goose-eating is celebrated in Germany and France on St. Martin's day. In Denmark, this festival is holden on the eve of
St. Martin, when every family (that can afford it) has a roasted
goose for supper. *Goose-feast* is a proverbial name for Michaelmas.

‡ *Twelve Moneths.* Lond. 1661, p. 44.

He that hath a good harvest may be content with
some thistles.

A blackberry (brambleberry) summer.*

No tree bears fruit in autumn,† that does not blossom
in the spring.

<hr>

September‡ blows soft,
Till the fruit's in the loft.

The Michaelmas moon,
Rises nine nights alike soon.§

<hr>

* A few fine days, at the close of this, or opening of the
following month, when the fruit of the bramble ripens. This
fruit is vulgarly known by the name of "bumblekite," in the
county of Durham. In that district of Yorkshire bordering upon
Leeds, they are called "black-blegs."

† The autumnal quarter commences on the 22nd September.

‡ September possesses one property which no other month can
lay a similar claim to, viz.: "that its xv day is, at least, six
times out of seven, a beautifully fine one." See Dr. Forster's
Per. Calendar.

§ The above rhyme describes a simple astronomical phenomenon which takes place at this season, and which is usually called
the *harvest moon.* The moon rising now nearly at the same time
for several nights when in her greatest splendour, and when her
light is considered as useful, both in drying the cut grain, and
lighting the husbandman to his usual labours, the phenomenon
impresses the mind, raising at the same time, as it ought to do,
sentiments of admiration and gratitude for the beneficent wis-
dom which planned an arrangement so useful to the inhabitants
of the earth.—*Chambers' Pop. Rhy. of Scot.* p. 39 (1842).

On Saint Matthee,*
Shut up the bee.

Blest be the day that Christ was born,
We've getten't *mell* of Mr. —— corn ;
Weel bound and better shorn.

   Hip, hip, hip, huzza, huzza.†

Blessed be the day our Saviour was born,
For Master ——'s corn's all well shorn ;
And we shall have a good supper to-night,
And a drinking of all, and a kirn! a kirn! a hoa!‡

The master's corn is ripe and shorn,
We bless the day that he was born ;
Shouting a kirn! a kirn! ahoa!§

Bless the day that Christ was born,
We've gettin 'twel and Mr. —— corn,
Weel shavern and shorn, &c., &c.‖

OCTOBER.

An October moon is call the "hunter's moon."

---

* September 21st.

† The *harvest-home* "*call*" in the county of Durham.

‡ The Northumbrian harvest-home call.

§ The harvest call peculiar to Glendale, a district in Northumberland.

‖ A harvest call used in the North Riding of the county of York.

Good October,* a good blast,
To blow the hogs acorn and mast.†

A soul-cake, a soul-cake;
God have mercy on‡ your soul,
For a soul-cake.§

---

* " On the days of SS. Barnabas, Simon, and Jude, a tempest often arises."—From an ancient Romish Calendar, in the late Mr. Brand's library. Formerly (although, not now), the anniversary of the day of SS. Simon and Jude (28th Oct.) was deemed as rainy and prognostical as that of Swithin. In Dodsley's old play of the *Roaring Girl*, a character therein says, "I know 'twill *rain* upon Simon and Jude's day." Again, " Now a continual Simon and Jude's rain beat all your feathers as flat down as pancakes."

The failure of a crop of ash-keys (the fruit of the ash), in some counties in England, is said to betoken death in the royal family.

† The fruit of the beech.

‡ *Varia.*—On all Christian souls.

§ In North Wales, there is a custom of distributing *soul* cakes on All Souls' day (2nd Nov.), at the receiving of which, the recipient prays to God to bless the donor's next crop of wheat. *Pennant's Manuscripts*, note. These cakes were baked on *Allhallow-even* (31 Oct.); and I hope that this will prove my sufficient excuse for introducing the triplet which appears in the text, and likewise the following " oulde couplett," to the notice of my readers, under this month:—

> "——— God save your *saul*,
> Beens and all."

This was repeated in retribution of the rich man's charity, received on this day, in the counties of Lancaster and Hereford.

Haly on a cabbage-stock, and haly on a bean,
Haly on a cabbage stock, to-morn's Hallow-e'en.*

Hey-how for Hallow-e'en,
When all the witches are to be seen ;
Some in black, and some in green,
Hey-how for Hallow-e'en !†

Dry your barley land in October,
Or you'll always be sober.‡

NOVEMBER.

St. Martin's little summer.§
Fat as a bacon-pig at Martlemas.‖

At Ripon, in Yorkshire, on this day, the good women used to
bake a cake for every one in the family; so this is generally
called cake-night.—*Gent. Mag.*, vol. lx, p. 719. I believe the
custom is partially continued.

* This proverb is peculiar to the 30th of this month. All-
hallow even is on the 31st.

† See Burns's beautiful poem *Halloween*, and its valuable and
highly interesting notes.

‡ *i. e.* without you attend to this dictum, you will have no
barley to convert into malt.

§ So called from *three* or *four* remarkably fine sunny days
which periodically occur about the festival of Saint Martin the
Apostle. 23rd Nov.

‖ This old form of the word (Martinmas) is still common in
the north.

This is *hanging month.*[*]

On the first of November, if the weather holds
    clear,
An end of wheat-sowing do make for this year.[†]

Pray to remember,
The fifth of November,
    The gunpowder treason and plot;
When the king and his train,
Had nearly been slain,
    Therefore it shall not be forgot!

November take flail,
Let ships no more sail.

An early winter,
A surly winter.

---

[*] It appears that this month has attained to some degree of
celebrity for suicidal acts; but whether that horrible precedence
is its due, I really am unable to decide. Those, therefore, who
are curious in the matter, and desirous of ascertaining if such
is really the fact, I must refer for information to county coroners,
and M.D.s in general.

[†] Tusser, in his *Five Hundred Pointes of Good Husbandrie*, 4to.
Lond. 1580, fol. 75, notices this authoritative precept or adage
almost in the same words :—

> " Wife, some time this weeks, if the weather hold clear,
> An end of wheat-sowing we make for this yeare;
> Remember you, therefore, tho' I do it not,
> The *seed-cake*, the *pasties*, and *furmentie-pot.*"

Many frosts and many thowes,
Make many rotten yowes (ewes).

DECEMBER.

A black Christmas makes a fat church-yard.

If the ice will bear a goose before Christmas, it will
not bear a duck afterwards.

A merry Christmas* and a happy new year.

The *twelve* days of Christmas.†

As white as driven snow on a winter's day.

As dark as a Yule midnight.

Everyday's no Yule-day,—cast the cat a castock. ‡

Yule, Yule! a pack of new cards and a Christmas *fule.*

A green Yule makes a fat kirk-yard.

Big as a Christmas pig!

It's good to cry Yule at another man's cost.

As many *mince pies* as you taste at Christmas, so many
happy months will you have.§

---

* An ancient mode of salutation, exchanged by friends when
they first meet during the current day (Christmas); and within
a limited period afterwards.

† See note on proverb, "The day of St. Thomas, the blessed
divine, &c.," under this month.

‡ The stump of a cabbage; and the proverb means much the
same thing as "Spare no expense, bring another bottle of *small
beer !*"

§ A trite observation general through the whole of Westmorland and Cumberland.

As bare as the birch at Yule even.*

A Yule feast may be quit at Pasche.†

Christmas comes but once a year.

Ghosts never appear on Christmas-eve.‡

Busy as an oven at Christmas.

---

* In allusion to the Christmas log. It is spoken of one in extreme poverty.

† *i. e.* "a Christmas feast may be paid again at Easter;" or, "One good turn deserves another."

‡ So says Shakspeare; and the truth thereof few, *now-a-days*, will call in question. Grose observes, too, that those born on Christmas-day *cannot* see spirits.

What a happiness this must have been seventy or eighty years ago and upwards, to those chosen few who had the good luck to be born on this day; when the whole world was so over-run with ghosts, boggles, bloody-bones, spirits, demons, ignis-fatui, fairies, brownies, bug-bears, black-dogs, spectres, spelly-coats,* scare-crows, witches, wizards, barguests, Robin-good-fellows, hags, night-bats, scrags, break-necks, fantasms, hob-goblins, hobhoulards, boggy-boes, dobbys, hobthrusts, fetches, kelpies, warlocks, mock-beggars, mumpokers, jemmy-burties, and apparitions, that there was not a village in England that had not its peculiar ghost! Nay, every lone tenement or mansion which could boast of any antiquity, had its boggle or spectre. The church-yards were all haunted. Every green lane had its boulder-stone, on which an apparition kept watch by night; every common had a circle of fairies belonging to it; and there was scarce a shepherd to be met with who had not seen a spirit!

---

* These were Scotch boggles: they wore garments of shells, which made a horrid rattling when they appeared abroad.

The day of St. Thomas, the blessed divine,*
Is good for brewing, baking, and killing fat swine.

St. Thomas's-day is past and gone,
And Christmas is most come,
  Maidens arise,
  And bake your pies,
And save poor tailor Bobby some.†

Winter-time for shoeing,
Peascod-time for wooing.‡

Bouncer, buckler, velvet's dear,
And Christmas comes but once a year;
Though when it comes it brings good cheer;
So farewell Christmas once a year.§

---

* Dec. 21. This, too, is the shortest day, and the commencement of the winter quarter. It is likewise the first day of the festival of all festivals—Christmas; which anciently continued without interruption from this day to the 2nd February, the feast of the purification of the blessed Virgin Mary; but Christmas-day, and the twelve days succeeding, were considered the most sacred to mirth and hospitality: hence the proverbial phrase, "The twelve days of Christmas."

A custom, I believe, still exists in some parts of England, of ringing a merry peal upon the bells of the parish-steeple on this day. It is called "ringing in Christmas."

† Halliwell's *Nursery Rhymes*, 4th ed. p. 220.

‡ See art. "Peascod," Halliwell's *Arch. Dict.* p. 610, and *Literary Gazette* for July 1846, p. 626.

§ See note on this proverbial saying, Halliwell's *Nursery Rhymes*, 4th ed. p. 44.

He's a *fule* that marries at *Yule*;
For when the bairn's to bear,
The corn's to shear.*

Make we mirth for Christ's birth,
And sing we Yule till Candlemas.

It's good crying Yule,
On another man's stool.†

If Christmas-day on a *Monday* fall,
A troublous winter we shall have all.

Yule, Yule, Yule, Yule!
Three puddings in a pule (pool),
Crack nuts and cry Yule!‡

---

* A meet companion for another adage given under June.

† The best note that I can give will, I trust, be considered sufficiently explanatory and well-fitted for the nonce, viz.:—

> "It is good to cry Yule at another man's cost."

‡ This was, I understand, some fifty years ago, a common "cry," in the counties of York and Durham, on the night of Christmas-day: but what the "*three puddings in a pule*" are intended to typify, I have never been able to discover, unless it be three plum puddings on a ponderous pewter dish, floating, as it were, in a "pule" of sweetened rum-sauce? (they convey the idea of its being an abstract). The command to "*crack* nuts" may be inferred from the following extract from a Christmas carol, given at the end of old George Wither's *Juvenilia*,—

> " Harke how the wagges abrode doe call
> Each other foorth to rambling;
> Anon, you'll see them in the hall,
> For *nuts* and apples scambling."

F

Hogmanay, trollolay;
Give us of your white bread,
But none of your grey.

Hagmena, Hagmena;
Give us cake and cheese,
And let us go away.*

Blessed be St. Stephen,
There's no fasting on his even !†

If you bleed your *nag* on St. Stephen's-day,‡
He'll work your *wark* for ever and ay !§

---

* This, and the preceding, partake more of the quality of
" crys," or chansons, than proverbs ; they were sung or said by
children on the last day of the year, when collecting their
" farls," as they named it, of *oaten cake* and *cheese*. See *Gent.*
Mag., vol. lx. p. 499.

† Happily expressive of the good eating and great doings at
this festive season.

‡ December 26th.

§ Hospinian quotes a superstitious notion from Naogeorgus,
which is thus translated by Barnaby Googe:—

> " Then followeth St. Stephen's day, whereon doth every man,
> His *horse* jaunt and course abrode, as swiftly as they can,
> Until they do extremely *sweate*, and then they let them *blood*.
> For *this* being done *upon this day*, they say doeth do ym good,
> And keeps ym from all maladies, and sicknesse through ye yeare,
> As if that *Steven* any time, tooke charge of *horses* heare."

Tusser, in his *Five Hundred Points of Good Husbandry*, under
December, says:—

> " Ther Christmas be passed, *let horsse be let blood*,
> For manie a purpose it dooth them much good:
> The day of St. Steeven, old fathers did use,
> If that doe mislike thee, some other day chuse."

Yule is come, and Yule is gone,
And we have feasted well;
So Jack must to his flail again,
And Jenny to her wheel.

An annotator on Tusser subjoins: "About Christmas is a *very proper time to bleed horses in*, for then they are commonly at house, then spring comes on, the sun being now coming back from the winter solstice, and there are three or four days of rest; and if it be upon *St. Stephen's day*, it is not the worse, seeing there are with it three days of rest, at least two."— *Tusser Redivivus*, 8vo. Lond. 1744. p. 148. In the *Receipts and Disbursements of the Canons of St. Mary in Huntingdon*, under the year 1517, we have the following entry:—

"*Item*, for letting our horses blede in Chrystmasse weke, iiijd."—*Nicholas's Illustrations of the Manners and Expenses of Ancient Times in England.*

According to one of Mr. Douce's manuscript notes, he thinks the practice of bleeding horses on this day is extremely ancient, and that it was brought into this country by the Danes. See *Olai Wormii Fasti Danici*, lib. ii. cap. 19.

Aubrey, in the *Remains of Gentilisme*, MS. Lands., Brit. Mus. 226, says: "On St. Stephen's day, the farrier came constantly and blouded all our cart-horses."

Bishop Hall, in his *Triumphs of Rome*, p. 58, says: "On St. Stephen's day, blessings are implored upon pastures."

In imitation of heathenism, the Romanists have assigned tutelar gods to distinct professions and ranks of people; nay even to the care of animals, thus:—

"St. Gartrude riddes the house of mise, and killeth all the rattes ;
The like doth Bp. Huldrich, w^h his earth two passing cattes."

Again:—

"And Loye, the smith, doth looke to horse, and smithes of all degre."

He likewise had the honour of attending to farriers and kine.

[Brydges

Summer in winter, and a summer's flood,
Never boded England good.

A frosty winter, and a dusty March,
    And a rain about Aperill;
And another about the Lammas time,
    When the corn begins to fill;
Is worth a plough of gold,
And all her pins theretill.

Bridges, in his *History of Northamptonshire*, vol. i. p. 258, says:
" In this church (Wedon Pinkeney) was the memorial of
St. Loy's kept, whither did many resort for the cure of their
horses ; where there was a house at the east end thereof,
plucked down within these few years, which was called St. Loy's
house."

Sir Thomas Overbury, in his *Characters*, when describing a
" running footman," among other matters, says, " His horses
are usually let bloud on St. Steven's day: on St. Patrick's, he
takes rest, and is drencht for all ye yeare after."

Melton, in his *Astrologaster*, p. 45, informs us, it was formerly
an article in the creed of popular superstition that it was not
lucky to put on a new suit of clothes, pare one's nails, or begin
anything on Childermas-day. Holy Innocents' day, 27 Dec.

Bourne tells us, chap. xviii., that, " according to the monks, it
was very unlucky to begin any work upon whatsoever day that
falls on, whether on the Monday, Tuesday, or any other, nothing
must be begun on that day through the year."

This is a black day in the calendar of impatient lovers.
None are ever married upon Childermas-day.

In the Orkney Islands, " no couple chooses to be married
except with a growing moon, and some even wish for a flowing
tide."— *Sir John Sinclair's Account of Scotland.*

ADDENDA.

A SONG FOR CHRISTMAS-DAY,

Curiously illustrative of one section of the popular belief relating to that day.

[From MS. Harl. No. 2252, fol. 153, r, of the 15th century.]

Yᴿ Crystmas day on the Sonday be,
A trobolus wynter ye shall see,
 Medlyd with waters stronge;
Were shalbe good wythoute fabylle,
The somer it shalbe resonabylle,
 And stormys odyr whylys amonge.

Wynus that yere shalbe goode,
The herveste shalbe wete wyth floddes,
Pestylens falle in many a contré,
And many younge pepylle dede shal be,
 Or that sekenes lynne,
 And grete tempestes ther-ynne.

Prynces that yere with iren shall dye,
And chaungynge of many lordes eye,
 Amonge knyghttes grete debate;
Many tydynges shal com to men;
Wyffes shalle wepen then,
 Bothe pore and grete estates.

The faythe then shalbe hurte truly,
For dyvers poyntes of heresy
 That then shall apere,
Throwe temptynge of the fende;
For diverse maters unkynde,
 Shalle cawse grete daunger.

Catelle shal threve one and odyr,
Save beeve, they shall kyll eche odyr,
 And som bestes shall dyen;
Little frute and corne goode,
No plenté of apylles to your foode;
 Shyppes on the see have payne.

That yere on the Monday, wythowte fyne,
Althynges welle thou mayste begynne,
  Hyt shalbe prophytabylle;
Chyldren that be borne that day,
Shalbe myghtye and stronge par fay,
  Of wytte full reasonnabylle.

A CHRISTMAS SONG,
Of import similar to the one preceding.
[From MS. Harl. No. 2252, fol. 154, rº.]

Lordynges, I warne yow al be-forne,
Yef that day that Cryste was borne
Falle uppon a *Sonday,*
That wynter shalbe good par fay,
But grete wyndes alofte shalbe
The somer shalbe fayre and drye;
By kynde skylle, wythowtyn lesse,
Throwe alle londes shalbe peas,
And good tyme all thynges to don;
But he that stelythe, he shalbe fownde sone;
Whate chylde that day borne be,
A grete lorde he shalle ge, &c.

Yf Crystemas day on *Monday* be,
A grete wynter that yere have shall ye,
And fulle of wyndes lowde and stylle ;
But the somer, trewly to telle,
Shalbe sterne wyndes also,
And fulle of tempeste al thereto ;
All catayle multyplye;
And grete plentye of beeve shall dye.
They that be borne that day, I wene,
They shalbe stronge eche on and kene ;
And he that stelythe owghte ;
Thow thowe be seke, thou dyeste not.

Yf Crystmas day on *Tuysday* be,
That yere shall dyen wemen plenté ;
And that wynter wex grete marvaylys ;
Shypps shalbe in grete perylles ;
That yere shall kynges and lordes be slayne,
And myche hothyr pepylle agayne heym.
A drye somer that yere shalbe ;

Alle that be borne therin may se,
They shalbe stronge and covethouse.
Yf thow stele awghte, thou lesyste thi lyfe ;
Thou shalte dye throwe swerde or knyfe ;
But and thow fall seke, sertayne
Thou shalte turne to lyfe agayne.

Yf Crystmas day, the sothe to say,
Fall uppon a *Wodnysday,*
That yere shalbe an harde wynter and strong,
And manye hydeus wyndes amonge ;
The somer mery and good shalbe ;
That yere shalbe wete grete plenté ;
Younge folke shall dye that yere also,
And shyppus in the see shal have gret woo.
What chylde that day borne ys,
He shalbe dowghtye and lyghte i-wysse,
And wyse, and slye also of dede,
And fynde many men mete and wede.

Yf Crystemas day on *Thursday* be,
A wyndy wyntyr se shalle yee,
Of wyndes and weders all wecked,
And harde tempestes stronge and thycke.
The somer shalbe good and drye,
Cornys and bestes shal multyplye :
That yere ys good londes to tylthe ;
And kynges and prynces shall dye by skylle.
What chylde that day borne bee,
He shalle have happe ryght well to the,
Of dedes he shalbe good and stabylle,
Of speche and tonge wyse and resonabylle.
Who so that day ony thefte abowte,
He shalbe shente wythowtyn dowte ;
And yf sekenes on the that day betyde,
Hyt shal sone fro the glyde.

Yf Crystmas day on the *Fryday* be,
The fyrste of wynter harde shalbe,
With froste and snowe and wyth flode,
But the laste ende thereof ys goode.
Agayn, the somer shalbe good also;
Folkes in hyr yen shall have grete woo;

Wemen wyth chylde, bestes, wyth corne,
Shall multyplye, and none be lorne.
The chylde that ys borne that day,
Shall longe lyve and lecherowus be aye.
Who so stelythe awghte, he shalbe fownde ;
And thou be seke, hyt lastythe not longe.

Yf Crystmas day on the *Saterday* falle,
That wynter ys to be dredden alle ;
Hyt shalbe so full of grete tempeste,
That hyt shall sle bothe man and beste ;
Frute and corne shall fayle grete won,
And olde folkes dyen many on.
Whate woman that day of chylde travayle,
They shalbe borne in grete peralle ;
And chyldren that be borne that day,
Within halfe a yere they shall dye, par fay.
The somer than shall wete ryghte ylle ;
Yf thou awghte stele, hyt shal the spylle ;
Thou dyest yf sekenes take the.

SIGNS OF FOUL WEATHER.

The *hollow winds* begin to blow,
The *clouds look black*, the *glass is low;*
The *soot falls down*, the *spaniels sleep*,
And *spiders* from their *cobwebs peep*.
Last night the *sun* went *pale to bed ;*
The *moon* in *halos* hid her head.
The boding *shepherd* heaves a sigh,
For, see a *rainbow* spans the sky.
The *walls are damp*, the *ditches smell*,
Clos'd is the pink-ey'd *pimpernel*.
Hark ! how the *chairs* and *tables crack*,
Old Betty's joints are on the rack :
Her corns with shooting pains torment her,
And to her bed untimely send her.
Loud *quack the ducks*, the *sea-fowl cry*,
The *distant hills* are *looking nigh*.
How restless are the *snorting swine !*
The *busy flies* disturb the *kine*.
Low o'er the *grass* the *swallow wings*,

The *cricket*, too, how *sharp he sings!*
Puss on the hearth, with velvet paws,
Sits *wiping* o'er her *whisker'd jaws.*
The *smoke* from *chimnies right ascends,*
Then spreading, *back to earth it bends.*
The *wind* unsteady *veers* around,
Or settling in the *south is found.*
Thro' the clear stream the *fishes rise,*
And *nimbly catch* the incautious *flies.*
The *glow-worms* numerous, clear and bright,
Illum'd the *dewy hill* last night.
At dusk, the squalid *toad* was seen,
Like *quadruped,* stalk o'er the green.
The *whirling-wind* the dust obeys,
And in the *rapid eddy* plays.
The *frog* has changed his *yellow vest,*
And in a *russet coat* is drest.
The *sky is green,* the *air is still,*
The mellow *blackbird's* voice is shrill.
The *dog,* so alter'd is his taste,
Quits mutton-bones, on *grass* to feast.
Behold the *rooks,* how odd their flight,
They imitate the *gliding kite,*
And seem *precipitate to fall,*
As if they felt the piercing ball.
The *tender colts on back do lie,*
Nor heed the traveller passing by.
In *fiery red* the *sun* doth *rise,*
Then *wades through clouds* to mount the skies.
　'Twill *surely rain!* we see't with sorrow,
No *working in the fields tomorrow!*
　　　　　　　　　　　　JENNER.

www.ingramcontent.com/pod-product-compliance
Lightning Source LLC
Chambersburg PA
CBHW020709270326
41928CB00005B/342